MOM'S DIARY

MOM'S DIARY

30 DAYS TO BEING A BETTER MOM

LYN ROSE

HOWARD
PUBLISHING CO.

3117 North 7th Street
West Monroe, LA 71291

Our purpose at Howard Publishing is:

- *Inspiring* holiness in the lives of believers
- *Instilling* hope in the hearts of struggling people everywhere
- *Instructing* believers toward a deeper faith in Jesus Christ

Because he's coming again

Mom's Diary
© 1994 by Howard Publishing Co., Inc.
All rights reserved

Published by Howard Publishing Co., Inc.
3117 North 7th Street, West Monroe, LA 71291-2227

First Printing, April 1994
Second Printing, July 1994
Printed in the United States of America

Cover Design by LinDee Loveland

ISBN#1-878990-30-6

Scripture quotations not otherwise marked are from the New International Version; © 1973, 1978, 1984 by International Bible Society. Used by permission Zondervan Bible Publishers.

To my own mother,
the sweetest example I could have,

to my daughters, Julie and Joy,
who give me plenty of opportunities to be a silly mom,

and *to my Young Mothers' Enrichment moms.*

(I appreciate you, too, Ron,
but this is *definitely* a "girl" book.)

CONTENTS

CONTENTS

PREFACE

As I reflect on my early years of motherhood, the memories become so much sweeter. It seems that the crying baby at 2 A.M., dirty diapers, chicken pox, and spilled orange juice fade into fuzzy oblivion after twenty years! I find myself stopping to smile and coo at babies in the malls and grocery stores. At church, I watch with wonder the toddlers who try so hard to whisper. Maybe it's just time for grandmotherhood.

Unfortunately, many young mothers are so busy, frazzled, and frustrated that they don't realize the small miracles their children bring every day. These moms don't realize that these really *are* the best years of their lives. But—good news— you don't have to wait until you are older and look back on motherhood to feel hope. This book offers help and inspiration.

Mom's Diary gives you thirty days toward being a better mom. Hopefully, my reflections will ease your tension in your current situation, perhaps change your perspective. I hope my journal will be the springboard to writing your own reflections that will make your mothering days sweeter. I hope *Mom's Diary* will help you set goals and priorities, encourage you in your high calling, uplift you in the good things you are doing. Some day, you'll love to look back on your writings and experience the memories becoming sweeter and share them with your grown children.

—Lyn Rose

Know that the Lord is God. It is he who made us, and we are his; we are his people, the sheep of his pasture.

Psalm 100:3

Rocking With Mom

Joy laid her face against my chest and settled close to me. She was my cuddler. Moments ago, she had awakened screaming, and her still frightened body shook with sobs.

But she was beginning to quiet now. As we rocked, intertwined as only a mom and her baby can be, her little body was soothed by my rhythmic motion with the rocker. Back and forth, back and forth. That calming movement is the language moms are best at. Sometimes I'd whisper or pat or rub or sing, but I never missed a swoosh of the rocking chair.

Joy must have felt the peace and security from me. "No need to fear, little one. I'm here now. It's okay." She closed her eyes and hugged her blankie as her thumb slipped into her mouth. "Yes, it's fine now. We can rock. Mom's here."

Our communication continued in the rocker for several more minutes. Joy calmed down and was nearly asleep. But I wasn't ready to put her back in her crib. I needed to rock some more. I wanted to savor this eternal moment, to feel my baby's spirit need me, and to know that her dad and I were the special ones God had chosen to raise her. As we cuddled, I realized I was the first one to teach her of God's great love. What an awesome honor and responsibility.

I thought of God's promises to me, that if I rest in him, casting my cares upon him, he will provide all I need. As my little one trusted so completely in me as we rocked, I recommitted my trust in my heavenly Father. I will rest in his promises.

So we rocked a little longer and I wondered, who is the rocking really for? Joy or Mom?

Dear Daughter,

Let the vacuuming wait one more day (you can pick up the big chunks by hand, if you must), hug your baby to your lap, rock, and read. Rocking is a lot more fun than vacuuming: better for your child, and even better for you.

Think how God must enjoy our running to him to spend time with him—reading his word, praying, or meditating. I imagine it feels like rocking. He must savor the warmth as I sit close to him and rest and enjoy comfort.

Our children, thriving in our comfort, model how we should be as heavenly children. Be alert to the many lessons your children can teach you, if you keep your eyes and heart open.

Love, Mom

DEAR LORD,

Thank you, Lord, for the rocking and the precious moments of connectedness with my child and you. Send me eternal moments to confirm my calling of motherhood. Sometimes I grow weary. Only you can bless me to know I'm in your will.

Through Jesus, Amen.

Reflections . . .

*For I have learned to
be content whatever the
circumstances. I know
what it is to be in need,
and I know what it is
to have plenty. I have
learned the secret of
being content in any
and every situation,
whether well fed or
hungry, whether living
in plenty or in want.*

Philippians 4:11b-12

Double Christmas

The frenzy of ripping open Christmas presents had slowed down, and Julie paused to look around the room. Destruction and devastation were everywhere. Torn boxes, crumpled wrapping paper, and discarded ribbons lay on the floor.

Julie had had a fantastic first Christmas—too, too many presents for an eleven-month-old to comprehend, but we didn't dare thwart the gift-giving spirit of the grandparents on their first grandchild's first Christmas.

As we all stopped for a breather, ready for eggnog in front of the fireplace, Julie readied herself for yet another round of Christmas.

She toddled over to the boxes and crumpled wrapping paper and began gathering them up. Then she plumped down on them and began Christmas all over. She investigated every box, tearing, ripping, throwing, chewing. Every box became a brand new toy, and she squealed as she tossed paper and ribbons into the air. Julie enjoyed another round of gifts. These were serendipities.

We tried to interest her in her new toys. "See, Julie, let's stack the blocks." "Oh, look at these little people in the schoolhouse." "Give your baby doll a hug." We parents and grandparents watched, amazed that our expensive, carefully chosen gifts had been overshadowed by the commonness of cardboard, paper, and ribbon. Julie felt content, even delighted, in these simple things.

Am I content in simple things? I reviewed my wants and desires and felt a little ashamed that I can always think of more I want, more I could use. Not a lusting and grabbing after worldly goods, but a "wouldn't it be nice if . . ." mindset. All too often I'm controlled by the world's viewpoint, not content in the bountiful things God has provided. When I want more and more, I'm not able to thank God for his gifts of family, friends, home, job, church, and nature. The world would have me discontent and unhappy with what I have. Thankfully, my child humbles me and brings me a fresh perspective.

Dear Daughter,

Be creative in the ways you teach simplicity to your kids. Notice the materials in your home that can be safe toys for your children. Let them play in your bottom kitchen drawer where you store the plastic containers or the pots and pans. Let them play in Dad's sock drawer (a good chance to practice putting away, too). Kids love to play with blankets and pillows. Make homemade playdough. Cut an old foam mattress into blocks. Finger-paint with pudding. Make mud pies outside. Cut and paste pictures out of magazines.

These activities may require more of your time, but they are simple and don't cost much money— only your investment in your child's imagination.

Remember that you model simplicity to your children. Simple habits and simple living will teach powerfully.

Love, Mom

DEAR LORD,

Open my eyes and help me see the simplicity and abundance you have lovingly provided. Let me rejoice in the pure beauties you show me: a raindrop on a flower, the glistening of light through my window, a spider's web, the laughter of my child. Let me live thankfully that I may teach my children your bounty.

In Jesus' name, Amen.

Reflections . . .

Rejoice in the Lord always.
I will say it again: Rejoice!
Let your gentleness be
evident to all.
The Lord is near.
Do not be anxious
about anything, but in
everything, by prayer and
petition, with thanksgiving,
present your requests to God.
And the peace of God, which
transcends all
understanding, will guard
your hearts and your minds
in Christ Jesus.

Philippians 4:4-6

Reveling in the Icing

Grandma and Grandpa pranced through the room with their paper party hats on, blowing their party whistles. Aunts and uncles "oohed" and "aahed" as they gathered around, cousins giggled and ran, proud parents smiled. Cameras flashed, as if the center of attention were a Hollywood star. We were a silly scene.

Joy's fingers first sampled a lick of chocolate frosting. She discovered, "M-m-m-m good!" With zest, she attacked her birthday cake with both pudgy hands. The birthday girl dug into the cake like digging in her sandbox in the back yard. She splashed around like she was in the bathtub, or maybe she was more like a puppy enthusiastically retrieving a buried bone.

I tried a bib to protect her new birthday dress (a pink and lace dream), but quickly realized what a losing proposition that was.

We had hoped for the classic "cake-on-the-face-first-birthday" picture. We got it. And more. We snapped "Joy and Mom," "Joy and Dad," "Joy and Grandma and Grandpa," and "Joy and Puppy Licking Frosting" for the photo shoebox.

What we really saved that day in our memory scrapbook was the celebration of Joy's addition to our lives. As family and friends, we reaffirmed God's gift to us—a soul precious to God, a little one entrusted to our care, but to be returned to our heavenly Father one day.

In the midst of a birthday celebration, I thought how serious our responsibility is for this child, and how thankful I am for God's gift of guidance as I parent. I was reminded to plead every day for God's continued blessing for our family.

Joy ate cake till she'd had her fill. She laughed and loved being the center of attention. She didn't celebrate with the depth of significance that we did. This milestone of one year of her life brings joy upon joy. Daughters are good at doing that!

Dear Daughter,

The big events are easy to celebrate. Try applauding "non-events" as if they were special days. Give a special treat because your child picked out a red shirt. Or honor Dad because he came home from work happy; he can sit on a special cushion at the dinner table and listen as you tell him how special he is. Take your child on a treasure hunt throughout the house following clues you have hidden. At the end, read a story as a reward. Or sing a silly song, changing the words and inserting your child's name—just for the fun of it. Practice saying yes more.

Celebrate the small successes: Set the table with flowers because your little one picked up her toys. When she can repeat a Bible verse, make a fancy crown for her to wear at the dinner table.

If I had it to do over again, I'd be a sillier mom.

Love, Mom

DEAR LORD,

Help me every day to celebrate at least one thing. Let me see your unique plan in everything. Especially let me embrace the wonder of my family and thank you daily for them. Teach me to enjoy the big events, and to make a big deal out of the little successes as well.

In Jesus' name, Amen.

Reflections . . .

Be still,
and know
that I am God;
I will be exalted
among the nations,
I will be exalted
in the earth.

Psalm 46:10

Ruffles and Lace

She looked like a Victorian baby, a little angel in ecru lace and ruffles upon ruffles. The dress had turned out beautifully, in fact, perfect.

I lost count of the hours I had sewn and smocked—maybe twenty-five, maybe forty—on a dress that an eighteen-month-old would outgrow in a few months.

At first, sewing frustrated me. It seemed that I spent more time ripping out mistakes than I did sewing the right seams. I thought I spent too much time running to my neighbor's so she could translate the pattern instructions and help me figure out what I had done wrong.

When I quit work just before Julie's birth, I promised I would watch expenses and cut corners. I figured sewing clothes for Julie would be a way I could help my husband ease the budget strain. But I wondered if I could keep up my end of the bargain. Cutting expenses and sewing, specifically, weren't as easy as I had imagined.

But as I gained more skill and confidence with sewing (and with many trips to my neighbor's), I began to enjoy the quiet task of working with fabric. My frustration eased, and my sewing became a prayer time. As I smocked on Julie's Victorian dress, I talked to God about my daughter and her future. I prayed for her health, her friends, her teachers, her study habits, her safety, her career, her husband, and especially her salvation.

As I sat at my machine, guiding the fabric, I prayed for my husband's and my parenting skills, for sensitivity to our developing child, for openness to her needs, for our family to be a family for God.

For me, sewing became more than a way of helping with our expenses. It became a time of deepening commitment to being God's woman. Sewing helped to slow me down so I could reflect on what I really wanted out of life. In those times of reflection, God impressed on my heart the desire to aim for his values and work toward them.

Dear Daughter,

It's hard, even impossible, for a mom of young children to find time to be alone with God, but taking time just for the two of you is so important. Time with God is revitalizing, rejuvenating, and energizing. During this quiet time God can directly touch you with his instructions.

You will be able to hear him say: "You're doing a great job, my child. Keep it up. I know it's hard at times, but know that you have my blessing. I'm here to help you every step of every day as you love your babies. You're doing the most important work of all."

Call it a "mental health holiday." Let your husband know you must lock the bathroom door and soak in the tub for a while or take the phone off the hook during the kids' nap so you can meditate and pray.

Sure, it'll take some creative effort to come up with a quiet fifteen or thirty minutes, but you're worth it!

Love, Mom

DEAR GOD,

Thank you that you know me best, and for providing the things best for me. But I need open eyes to see your guidance and to follow your bidding.

I may not notice that you're trying to slow me down to think on eternal values. I may not understand your plan in slowing me down, but please keep on nudging me until I learn.

In Jesus' name, Amen.

Reflections . . .

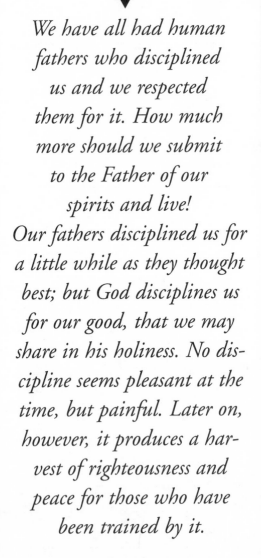

We have all had human
fathers who disciplined
us and we respected
them for it. How much
more should we submit
to the Father of our
spirits and live!
Our fathers disciplined us for
a little while as they thought
best; but God disciplines us
for our good, that we may
share in his holiness. No dis-
cipline seems pleasant at the
time, but painful. Later on,
however, it produces a har-
vest of righteousness and
peace for those who have
been trained by it.

Hebrews 12:9-11

"No No"

As two-year-old Joy eyed the china tea set on the coffee table, I knew what was coming. (Moms know these things.) Her eyes twinkled as she made a beeline straight for her aunt's "play pretties" from London.

I grimaced with foreknowledge and said a prayer. A lesson to be learned was on its way. (Moms know these things, too.)

Joy's big eyes viewed the scene expectantly— the shining gold on the teapot caught her eye. The sparkling treasure waited to be claimed.

She hesitated, as if she remembered Mom's warning, "Just touch with your eyes." But Joy's kid-reasoning overruled Mom's: "Just one touch with one finger can't hurt."

Before I could reach her, Joy had one fragile cup in both hands, caressing it, pretending to take a drink like a grown-up lady at tea.

After a firm "no," I took the cup from her and put it down. I diverted her attention to a wooden puzzle, but in three minutes she was back handling the tea set.

A firm slap on her hand came with my "no." We repeated the attempted diversion and the ensuing slap several times. Joy's determination persevered. But I was bigger, I told myself, and she had to learn what "no" meant.

Finally, we went outside to play, the ultimate diversion. I'm not sure who "won," but I felt she had gotten the "no" message.

I thought of how determined I must look in my sinning. Repeatedly, God points me back to the right path, even places me on it firmly, sometimes slapping my hand, but I keep reaching for the forbidden. I choose to err. How loving is my Father's reprimand. He knows I need discipline to keep me on the path. He knows I need lots of people sent my way to remind me of the right path.

Dear Daughter,

There will be many times when the "no nos" bring tears, and you'll feel like the "heavy" or the "hit man." Hang in there! This training for your children is necessary. It is God-given and God-ordained. You are the one to teach God's principles.

But there are other times when it is more constructive to remove the temptation from the child. The temptation of the gold tea set might be too great, and it would be easier for all involved to put the tea set on top of the refrigerator.

There will be several years during toddlerhood when china and crystal are stored behind locked doors, but, rest assured, there will be plenty of later years when your "play pretties" can boldly sit out on coffee tables. That is, until the grandkids come!

Love, Mom

DEAR FATHER,

Help me to learn my lessons quickly. Continue to be patient with me in my correction. I yearn to be like you, and I realize that it'll take a long time. So don't give up on me. I know you won't.

In Jesus' name, Amen.

*R*eflections . . .

Oh, how I love your law! I meditate on it all day long.
How sweet are your words to my taste, sweeter than honey to my mouth!
Your word is a lamp to my feet and a light for my path.

Psalm 119:97, 103, 105

Mule With a Tyke Bike

J ulie screamed and pulled with all her two-year-old might. From the other end of the new Tyke Bike, Dad gently urged, "Daddy has to put it together for you first. Let Daddy have it. I'll give it back. Promise!"

No way!

The Norman Rockwell picture-perfect Christmas scene of our family gathered around the tree opening presents had been shattered with Julie's cries, "No! Daddy! Mine!" No amount of soothing comments or rationalization could convince her that she should relinquish her iron-fast grip on the Christmas bike. Her stubborn face reddened with commitment and a singular focus.

She would not give up easily. For fifteen more minutes she retained her grip on the new bike, while her father attached handle bars and wheels. All the time, her hand claimed the new present as hers.

I wondered, to what things do I cling so tenaciously? Do I attack spiritual concerns with Julie's resolution and headstrong determination? Do I cling tightly to God's Word? Do I daily grasp his promises securely in my heart? It doesn't matter if Satan and the world whisper, "It's okay to let go for just a second. It won't hurt. You can always come back later. Trust me." I must dig in my heels, grit my teeth, and, like Julie, scream loudly, "No! They're mine! I need God's precious promises for life!"

Dear Daughter,

Maybe you'll have a daughter with a stubborn streak, and maybe you'll have lots of wars of the will. If so, you will have many opportunities to investigate the inner workings of your child.

I want to urge you to look beyond the surface problem to your child's feelings that may be at the root of the behavior. First, sit in the floor so you'll be on the same level as your little one, and talk to her and help her describe her feelings. Get her to tell how she's acting. Perhaps playing out the scene with dolls will help your child describe her feelings. Distracting her attention from the immediate battle should defuse some of the explosive emotions.

Try to channel her energy in positive ways: work on a puzzle, read a story to her dolls, or have a tea party for all her teddy bears. You'll discover treasures of strength in your strong-willed child. Praise God for your child and these challenges.

Love, Mom

DEAR GOD,

Just as my child clings to a toy with an "It's mine!" attitude, I will hang on to your promises. I know your word is true and good and as sweet as honey. Help me to cling to your promises.

In Jesus' name, Amen.

Reflections . . .

*And we, who with
unveiled faces all
reflect the Lord's
glory, are being
transformed into
his likeness with
ever-increasing
glory, which comes
from the Lord,
who is the Spirit.*

2 Corinthians 3:18

Sweet When They're Asleep

"They're so sweet when they're asleep." Haven't I heard that a million times? Yet it remains true. When I peek in at that curly, blond-headed little girl at night when she's asleep, all I see is the sweet spirit God put in her. My innocent child, placed in the safety of my care, sleeps in sweet abandon that all is well in the world. She lies there trusting that God is in control. She reminds me that the Lord is shaping all of us into his eternal glory; he has promised, and he is able.

The half-smile of contentment on my child's face holds no reminders of the day's shenanigans. Who could guess that this same sweet girl had earlier christened the kitchen wallpaper with oatmeal, tried to flush the cat down the toilet, spilled three glasses of grape juice, and beat the neighbor boy over the head with her Fisher Price school bus? And that was just before 10:00 A.M.

In his great wisdom, God knew that moms need a reprieve from each day's endless activities.

He knew that we need to sneak at least one look at a peaceful, sleeping face each day, lest we forget that there is an angel within our roaming, raging toddler. How wise of our heavenly Father to put our child to sleep at night so we could have a brief, eternal look at the soul within our child. These peeks help us put things in perspective.

We realize that our daily task of mothering is not about the cleaning, cooking, and straightening. Our job is an eternal one of leading our families closer to God. We lead our little ones to Jesus as we show Christ-like love, patience, joy, and peace in our daily lives of mothering. Gain strength and confidence in knowing that God has ordained you with the highest calling. He's called us to be Jesus to our family. Often we may focus on the wrong things and get "out of whack" during the day, but then, fortunately, rest time comes, when we can get a little peek at that sweet child asleep and reground our priorities.

Without these refreshing moments of re-creation, we would become too easily burdened with the putting up, the folding, the cleaning, the "no nos," the interruptions of our daily routine.

Thank the Lord for these times when we can sense the wisdom of the eternal scheme and feel our part in our child's life. We gain strength, perspective, and peace from seeing our child asleep at night. We can almost see God at work on our child as he continues to change us all into his glory.

They are sweet when they're asleep, aren't they?

Dear Daughter,

I remember many times when I was on the brink of strangling your little neck or tying you in your chair, and you were saved only by the grace of your naptime.

I would urge you to have regular get-togethers with other moms so you can share experiences and learn from each other. Form a support group. A poll found that the most stressful job in the world is raising two children under the age of five. Sharing with other moms will give you helpful insight, but mostly you will realize that others are going through experiences similar to yours and that you're normal. Your feelings of anger, frustration, and inadequacy will be understood as you meet with these other moms. These times of sharing will bring refreshment to your spirit and strength to carry on joyfully.

And don't forget to look in at your sleeping baby for more sweet refreshment, coming straight from your heavenly Father.

Love, Mom

DEAR LORD,

Help me keep my mothering in eternal perspective. Help me not to get caught up in the daily, mundane tasks that are unrelenting and so demanding. Rather help me to focus on the eternal values I am modeling daily for my family. Give me many moments of sneaking peeks at the eternal angels within my children.
Through Jesus, Amen.

Reflections . . .

Create in me a pure heart,
O God, and renew a
steadfast spirit within me.
Do not cast me from your
presence or take your Holy
Spirit from me. Restore to
me the joy of your salva-
tion and grant me a will-
ing spirit, to sustain me.
The sacrifices of God are a
broken spirit; a broken
and contrite heart, O God,
you will not despise.

Psalm 51:10-12, 17

Dancing Corn

J oy smiled sweetly at me, then looked at her dinner plate—chicken strips, peas, and corn. She had picked at it grudgingly for most of the dinner hour.

My overdose of syrupy persuasion had failed; I recognized that gleam in her eye. It signaled that my cajoling had surpassed its usefulness, and disaster was imminent.

Her jaws firmly set and her teeth tightly clenched, she grabbed the plate and calmly flipped its contents over the side of the high chair. With a flourish of her fingertips, she let go of the plate. It crashed to the floor. The dancing corn and peas shot across the room; the chicken strips merely plopped on the linoleum.

Her furrowed brow emphasized her defiance. She wasn't going to eat her dinner! She had made up her mind! My gentle prodding and clever tactics were in vain.

How does my defiance look to God? Joy's defiant face is not pretty as it brings to mind the many times I have acted similarly toward God. My own defiance is not a pretty picture. There have been times when I have felt God's leading in a direction of Bible study or service, but instead of answering his call warmly, I have clenched my jaw as an affront to God and said "no" through my gritted teeth. "I think my ways are better, God," my attitude says. Many times I have not confessed my attitude of self-righteousness, my spoken unkindnesses, or my acts of injustice.

How my defiance must hurt God. How his heart must ache over me. He knows the very best plan for my life and sends to me the experiences to honor that plan. He must hurt when I choose to ignore him.

As an obedient child, I need to unclench more, say yes to his leading, yield to his plan, and follow joyfully and thankfully.

Dear Daughter,

When defiance attacks you, re-cognize it and call it by its name. Take the offensive. Don't play "religious" and make excuses for yourself. Don't pretend to be spray painted with holiness, but admit your defiance to his will. Pray to God and confess that you don't want to do what he's calling you to do. You don't feel like going where he's leading. Only then can God work on you. If you're willing to change your attitude, God's Spirit will change you.

Consider this same procedure for your children's defiance. Don't over-react with anger when they express defiance, but help them understand what they're feeling so you can help them change. Tell them that it's okay to feel angry, but it isn't acceptable to throw food, throw a temper tamtrum, or refuse to pick up toys. Say, "I'm sorry you don't want to pick up the blocks. Sometimes cleaning up isn't fun." You might offer a small treat as a reward, offer to help, or set the timer for five minutes to help them complete the tasks.

Love, Mom

DEAR LORD,

Soften my heart to respond to you willingly. I don't want the look of defiance to harden on my face. Encourage me when I do step out in faith, unsure of myself and unsure of you. Reward me in my little steps toward trusting you more.

In Jesus' name, Amen.

Reflections . . .

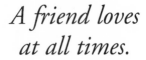

*A friend loves
at all times.*

Proverbs 17:17a

*There is a friend
who sticks closer
than a brother.*

Proverbs 18:24b

*If one falls down,
his friend can
help him up.*

Ecclesiates 4:10a

They Were Only Small Bites

We had just moved to our new home in a new town, and I had only one new friend. She was kind enough to offer to keep two-year-old Joy while I ran necessary moving-in errands.

When I returned, I noticed that her son Mark was crying, and the two kids were separated.

"What happened?" I asked.

"I think Mark didn't share what he was playing with. I noticed these little marks on his arm, and I think Joy may have bitten him. Don't worry about it; the kids are all right."

My friend was so low-key about the incident that I followed her cue and thought "no big deal."

Through the months, Mark and Joy spent many afternoons together as my friend or I would run errands. Our friendship developed into a deep one, and our hearts connected in a special way.

A couple of years later, we were remembering my first days in town and my adjustment to the move. We got to laughing about Joy's biting Mark that first time they were together.

My friend let it slip that that incident wasn't the only time. Joy bit Mark often on her visits.

I was horrified, "You mean, Joy bit all the time and you never told me?"

My friend assured me that they were "only little bites." She figured Joy was expressing her insecurity about the new surroundings, and Mark just happened to get in the way of her teeth. Their friendship never suffered.

And neither did ours. She was a true friend to realize that some things seem small (they were only small bites) in comparison to the value of a growing relationship. She nurtured our friendship knowing that her son suffered some at the grip of Joy's teeth. Our friendship blossomed into an enduring relationship, one that has weathered two more moves. We can still laugh about the bites.

◆

Dear Daughter,

You may think that being a friend comes naturally, but it doesn't always. Social skills may need nurturing in some children. Plan a variety of settings for your child to experience friendship: one-on-one at the park for a picnic, two or three over to play games, a few over to see a movie, a mom and her child over to eat lunch. Let your child interact with outgoing kids as well as quiet ones.

After the guests go home, you and your child can talk about different friends and all the different kinds of people God created. Stress that God made each of us different, so he must really like variety and a lot of fun.

Love, Mom

DEAR LORD,

Thank you for true friends who see beyond the surface to the deeper values inside, for friends who show grace and forgiveness even though we don't ask for it. Help me be that kind of friend.

In Jesus' name, Amen.

Reflections . . .

_____

_____

_____

_____

_____

_____

_____

_____

_____

_____

◆

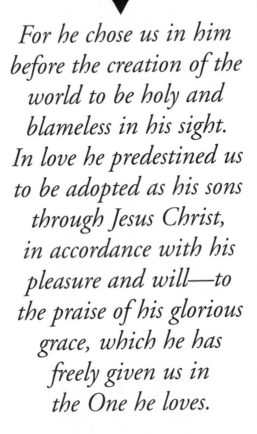

*For he chose us in him
before the creation of the
world to be holy and
blameless in his sight.
In love he predestined us
to be adopted as his sons
through Jesus Christ,
in accordance with his
pleasure and will—to
the praise of his glorious
grace, which he has
freely given us in
the One he loves.*

Ephesians 1:4-6

Love With Sticky Fingerprints

She had carefully traced the heart pattern, and now Julie's chunky little hands gripped the scissors with focused energy. Her teeth pressed into her lower lip as she concentrated fully on cutting out the red construction paper heart. I could hear her breathing out loud. Her concentration was mind boggling! Her hands could hardly control the scissors, but she was trying with all her strength. She was nearly finished with her choppy three-year-old-style cuts. I offered some help, but Julie insisted on doing it by herself.

Then came the best part: glueing. Julie squeezed out the glue, outlining the back side of the heart, then snaked lots of glue in designs (the really fun part). Slowly and deliberately she picked up the heart by its sides and flipped it over.

"Mommy, do you think Grandma Sibyl will like my card?"

"Oh, yes, honey," I assured her. "I know Sibyl will be surprised, and she will love your card."

Our family had gotten to know Sibyl when we first moved to our new town and new church. Sibyl was recently widowed, and her children did not live close by. Ours was an instant bonding, one that enriched our family.

Sibyl helped Julie learn to love others outside our family and show honor and respect to other adults. Julie practiced being a servant and helping Sibyl. She often wanted to share baked treats with Sibyl, and after we'd potted flowers, we usually had to drive over to Sibyl's to take her some. Julie helped me set the table extra special when Sibyl joined us for dinner.

The choppy red heart decorated the white folded card. Inside Julie and Mom wrote, "Happy birthday, Grandma Sibyl. I love you."

Julie beamed as she handed the card to Sibyl, her special "adopted" Grandma. The card had a few gluey thumbprints on one side, the bottom edge was crinkled, but the message spoke loudly: "Love to you, Grandma Sibyl. You're a special person in my life."

I would guess that the construction paper card meant more to Sibyl than anything we could have bought her, and I know the lessons Julie learned are more precious than gold.

Dear Daughter,

You may feel overwhelmed with your work at home and outside the home and feel that you don't have time to get out and minister. In addition to the valuable ministry you do for your family, there are ways you can serve others that don't require lots of time. You can be an outreach minister, even after you've had a long day at work.

Don't get so busy that you don't take time to write cards and notes to people you care about. You don't have to use expensive cards or stationery; simply a message of love and concern on plain paper can mean so much to someone going through a difficult time. Try baking two loaves of bread and giving one as a gift. You can keep another mother's children on Saturday so she can go to the grocery store. You can commit to a ministry of intercessory prayer.

I keep a B.D.F (Bad Day File) which contains notes of encouragement I have received through the years. When I'm having an especially bad day and need to remember better times, I go to my files and read some of the letters. Those notes continue to boost me up as I read about the way I've touched people. A B.D.F. can be good medicine for your soul. Why don't you start your own B.D.F.?

Love, Mom

DEAR LORD,

It's wonderful to consider how you have chosen me to be your adopted daughter. Though I had no merit of my own, you poured out your love on me. You adopted me. Help me to live like it makes a difference. In Jesus' name, Amen.

$\mathcal{R}$eflections . . .

_____

_____

_____

_____

_____

_____

_____

_____

_____

◆

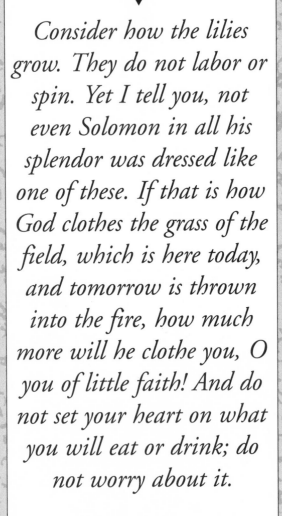

Consider how the lilies grow. They do not labor or spin. Yet I tell you, not even Solomon in all his splendor was dressed like one of these. If that is how God clothes the grass of the field, which is here today, and tomorrow is thrown into the fire, how much more will he clothe you, O you of little faith! And do not set your heart on what you will eat or drink; do not worry about it.

Luke 12:27-29

The Swinger

Standing up, Joy gripped the ropes with both hands. As she leaned back and arched her back and dipped her head, she swung with full force on the "big swing." Her long hair sailed out in back of her. She practiced these new movements methodically, and soon she gathered more momentum and power.

At first, her giggles were only tentative, perhaps because she was slightly afraid of this new-found flight, but before long, her loud squeals of delight called me to the kitchen window.

My first reaction was to yell, "Get down from there! Are you crazy? You're too little to stand up on the big swing! You're going to fall!" And I almost started running toward her to rescue her.

But then I noticed: she didn't need rescuing. I could see her confidence and skill growing in this moment of challenge. Joy wasn't afraid, but seemed quite comfortable swinging to fifteen-foot heights. She was almost flying! I decided to watch and not rush out to save her. I prayed for God to put a safety net under her, just in case her new swinging skills left her momentarily.

That day I witnessed the birth of the daredevil skills of our talented gymnast.

Joy's childlike abandon in her swinging had no room for mistrust and hesitancy. She never doubted that the swing would hold her. She gave herself up totally to the swinging motion, with no worry or fretting.

She made me think how often I fret about petty concerns and worries, not allowing myself to trust God's care fully. I worry too much about my children, our finances, where we'll live, if the car will make it. He has promised to take care of me, but I'm afraid. I need to "let go" and let him hold me up and be my strength.

Once I claim God's promises, I can swing with full force, empowered by the Holy Spirit.

Dear Daughter,

Teach your little girl she can do whatever she wants. Help her master the skills she wants to learn. Praise her for trying, and praise her even more when she succeeds. Years from now, she will still hear your applause.

Let her know it's okay to take risks. If she wants to try out for the softball team but is fearful she's not good enough, urge her to give it her best. Let her know that life's best experiences come from taking chances. She'll never know the fun of the softball team if she never tries.

Most importantly, let your daughter know that you're her mom and that no matter what—win or lose—you'll always love her.

Love, Mom

DEAR FATHER,

Just as I flop down on the couch at night when I'm exhausted, let my heart wholeheartedly rest in your care. Let me learn from the way you are caring for my little one. Teach me trust in the little things, that I may trust you in everything.

In Jesus' name, Amen.

Reflections . . .

She speaks with wisdom,
and faithful instruction
is on her tongue.

Proverbs 31:26

The fear of the Lord
is the beginning of
wisdom; all who follow
his precepts have good
understanding. To him
belongs eternal praise.

Psalm 111:10

Look, Mom!

"Come here, Mommy. Come here and see what I did!"

As I walked into Julie's room, I could see her smiling proudly as she stood at the foot of her bed.

"See, Mommy, I made my bed all by myself!" She looked up at me, asking for approval.

"Oh, Julie. That's wonderful. You did such a great job. You must have worked very hard. I appreciate you. We'll have to be sure and show Dad. I'm so glad you're my little girl!"

A quick hug and she bounded away, on to the next event in a busy three-year-old's life.

The bedspread must have hidden half the toys she owned, as the lumps made a small Rocky

Mountain range. Sure enough, I could see Raggedy Ann's leg sticking out of the tucked-up bedspread, and Joy's pink elephant was half hidden under the pillow. A mother would certainly have done the job differently. My corners would have been perfectly square, no lumps in my bed.

I held back my maternal urge to straighten her bed. In the golden moment while Julie anticipated my response to her accomplishment, her little soul lay bare, awaiting Mother's comments. Would they be positive and uplifting or negative and pull her down?

Moms receive special strength from the heavenly Father to zero in on these opportune moments. Somehow we are given discerning eyes to examine our child's heart to know what she needs. "Yes, Julie, that's a super job!"

Praise for a job well done, comfort for a hurt, joy for an accomplishment, tears for a pain, and lots of hugs and kisses for all times. Moms just know these things.

Dear Daughter,

Start giving your little ones jobs to do when they are small. Help a toddler learn to pick up toys or straighten the videos. An older child can pick up clothes, make his bed, take out small trash baskets, set out the napkins and forks. Remember to give lots of praise for the efforts (and maybe nickels, dimes, and quarters).

Though it is hard for you to be disciplined and to stick with the training regimen, know that you will reap fruitful rewards later as you see your children handle larger responsibilities successfully.

Love, Mom

DEAR LORD,

I give you praise, my Father, for this motherly insight. You, who have all wisdom and knowledge, see fit to give me a little bit of your knowledge so I can guide my children. Thanks. I need all the help I can get!

Through Jesus, Amen.

Reflections . . .

Pleasant words are a honey-comb, sweet to the soul and healing to the bones.

Proverbs 16:24

Whatever is true, whatever is noble, whatever is right, whatever is pure, whatever is lovely, whatever is admirable—if anything is excellent or praiseworthy— think about such things.

Philippians 4:8

Dandelion Bouquets

The picture could have come off a greeting card: out of focus, slightly fuzzy, a girl with long, golden curls, arms outstretched, flash-stopped in mid-run toward Mom.

Joy held a small bouquet of dandelions she had picked, and behind her was a wispy trail of downy dandelion seeds. Her smile spread proudly across her pudgy cheeks.

"Do you like them, Mom? Aren't they pretty? I picked them just for you."

"I sure do, honey," I said, hugging her. "Let's go put them in a vase. Oh, they're so pretty. You're my sweet girl!"

I put the dandelions (what was left of them— mostly stems with stubby heads) in a crystal vase in a place of honor on the kitchen table.

I accepted her gift as I accepted her outpouring of love for me. My first inclination, however, was to launch into a botanical lecture on how the feathery tips of the dandelion were really seeds and how we shouldn't blow on the flowers and spread the seeds because we don't want weeds to come up in our yard.

Instead I sighed and thought, "No matter how industriously we work in the yard, we always seem to have dandelions. So why not accept them and try to look at them through Joy's eyes? They do make a lovely, delicate bouquet."

I love the way my daughter accepts things, people, and situations pretty much as they are. She's not frustrated in trying to find the ideal or the perfect. She finds beauty everywhere. Where she finds dandelions, she finds a gift for Mom.

She helps me realize my world will not be perfect, but with God's strength I can learn a different perspective and use his eyes to look for the good and the beautiful.

It's true that we will always have dandelions, so why not make a bouquet?

Dear Daughter,

Be aware of how tender young hearts are. Your child wants so much to please you, probably more than anything else in the world.

You used to run in the house so glad to see me, so glad to be welcomed with hugging arms. Be sure always to have an encouraging greeting for your little one. First words should be positive and uplifting. Let your little one know you're glad she came home to you (or just came in from the backyard).

Embrace with thankfulness the gifts your child brings. Don't ever risk crushing a tender heart by careless criticism. Her fragile ego cannot take much negative input.

Be a well-spring of encouragement for your child, for the world yearns to tear her down.

Love, Mom

P.S. Husbands need to hear positive words, too.

DEAR FATHER,

Give me a positive perspective, like my child's, to see the small wonders in your creation. I want to be one who always brings out the best. Give me open eyes and discerning lips so that I will always be a joy to those around me.

I want to be like Jesus.

In his name, Amen.

Reflections . . .

*Do not forget
to entertain
strangers,
for by so doing
some people
have entertained
angels without
knowing it.*

Hebrews 13:2

Baking With Angels

I remember the scene: Flour on the floor, flour on the chair, flour on the countertop, and flour all over Julie. The mommy-sized apron hung baggy on her little four-year-old frame, but she was a big girl, making cookies with Mom.

"This is big girl work, Mommy," Julie said, carefully measuring and dumping in the sugar and flour. She wiped her hair from her face, dusting more flour across her forehead and cheeks. Mixing the stiff dough was especially tough for a four-year-old, so hard that I had to complete the final stirring with the big wooden spoon.

Daughter industriously rolled out the sugar cookie dough, placing the star cookie cutter on the dough and pressing firmly. Ah, there it was! A perfect star cookie—all ready for the cookie sheet. Julie methodically repeated her task, with the gingerbread boy, the heart, the circle, and the flower, until the cookie sheet was full and ready for the oven.

After the cookies baked, I ceremoniously took them from the oven for Julie's inspection. She gave them a hearty okay. "Oh, Mom, they're perfect! Won't Daddy be surprised? Won't Daddy be proud of me?"

At the end of the day, I wondered what I had accomplished. Flour was all over the kitchen, toys were scattered on the living room floor, the laundry was only half done, with clean towels piled on the couch waiting to be folded. Lunch, dinner, and cookie dishes were stacked on the counter waiting to go into the dishwasher. I was exhausted.

In my heart, though, I knew I had climbed a mountain and triumphed. The heart of my child had been made glad because I spent most of the day with her baking cookies. Daughter Julie learned that today baking cookies was more important than housework or errands. Just for today, I was all Julie's.

◆

Dear Daughter,

I hope you'll remember with fondness those special cookie days we had together. As I reflect, I think I worried too much about the household tasks that didn't get done and the flour all over the kitchen. I wish I had more often seized the moment and enjoyed our cookie time together with your childlike joy.

You still talk about our tradition of Christmas cookie baking. I doubt that you noticed that the housework didn't get done on cookie days. You didn't notice there was laundry to do, errands to run, and vacuuming to complete. But, really, what did that housework matter? Julie in a too-large apron, standing in a chair to reach the counter, Mom's arms encircling her, helping her measure the flour – that's what's important. That's what remains. The special time with Mom goes into the memory bank.

There are other blessings from a cookie baking day: the patience the child learns from measuring and mixing the ingredients carefully, the diligence learned from a hard job done well, and the self-esteem that comes from Mom and Dad's bountiful praise.

So, remember now to take time out for lots of cookie-baking days with your kids, whether these days be at Christmas or birthdays or just ordinary days. You might be baking with angels.

Love, Mom

DEAR LORD,

Help me determine to take special time alone with my children. Let me know that the housework will always be there, but my children will not always be. Slow me down to realize the eternal value of time spent with my daughters. I know you desire me to enjoy this time with my kids.

In Jesus' name, Amen.

Reflections . . .

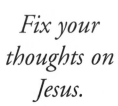

*Fix your
thoughts on
Jesus.*

Hebrews 3:1

Copy Cat

Big sister's clothes hung on little Joy. The sleeves drooped and totally hid her hands, and the dress hem dragged the ground. She flopped about in shoes too big, but Joy thought she looked great in big sister Julie's clothes. I had repeatedly told Joy to stay out of her sister's room. Julie would tell Joy almost daily to keep out of her "stuff," but to no avail.

Some may have called it curious exploration (and it may have been), but I saw hero worship in action. Little sister wanted so much to be like big sister that she would risk getting into trouble just so she could try out being Julie—wearing Julie's clothes, touching her "stuff," playing with her toys, wearing her hair bows.

Often I saw this hero worship in copycat actions. Joy used big sister's speech phrases, especially the, "Oh, Mom," of her mature six-year-old sister. Joy had stopped eating brussels sprouts because Julie once called them "monkey heads." Joy wanted her bangs feathered back and sprayed stiff like Julie's.

I wonder if big sister Julie realized that little eyes were on her all the time? She probably thought little sisters were a dreaded curse to be endured. But I saw a slowly growing relationship which would deepen through the years, from the early toleration of the pesky copycatting to a deepening admiration and friendship.

Whom do I copy? Am I coy or forthright in my behavior? Do I copy the actions of my older brother Jesus? Do I desire to be so much like him that I put him on every day? Just think, I bring Jesus honor when I copycat him, just as Julie must have been pleased when she realized that Joy wanted to be like big sis.

Dear Daughter,

You will copy the people you're around, whether conscious of it or not. So be sure to surround yourself with godly women, especially elder women who have solid Christian families. Their examples will model for you what God's woman should be like. You will unconsciously absorb their values and actions.

I have lived most of my adult life in towns far away from my mother, so everywhere we have lived, I have searched out an elder woman to be my special close friend or mentor. God has blessed me with Lavorise, Mary Jean, Kathleen, Rose, Patsy, and Barbara, who have shown me how to be a mother and wife. I urge you to do the same. Search out that older woman to mentor you into the likeness of Christ.

Love, Mom

DEAR LORD,

Instill in me the yearning to copy Jesus and to be like him in every way. Help me to pattern Jesus in service to my family. Let my following you spring from pure motives so others may see Jesus in me.

In his name, Amen.

Reflections . . .

◆

He gives strength to the weary and increases the power of the weak. Even youths grow tired and weary, and young men stumble and fall; but those who hope in the Lord will renew their strength. They will soar on wings like eagles; they will run and not grow weary, they will walk and not be faint.

Isaiah 40:29-31

Maiden on Wheels

The menacing two-wheeler stood proudly in the driveway, threatening to take my five-year-old daughter into unknown roads of independence. I felt shaky. I realized that as I guided Julie into this new-found freedom, my motherly "hold" would diminish.

In my head, I understood that Julie had to grow up. These developmental stages of growth are normal and are what we moms pray for. We brag proudly of every minor accomplishment. "She's already walking." "She knows her ABCs." "She can make her bed." "Want to see her tie her shoes?" But just seeing her sit on the two-wheeler makes the separation painfully clear as my little one rides on her symbolic first trip away from me.

Like most of these steps of growth, this feat of independence wasn't instantaneous. Her father and I ran by her side for at least five hundred miles, holding, steadying, guiding, and cheering her on.

"That's it! Great! Lean this way. Look straight ahead. Can you balance? Do you feel it? Now you've got it! Wow, Julie, look at you!"

Only a few falls and minor scrapes tarnished her maiden voyage. As we finally let go and stood back to watch her ride off on her own, her dad and I smiled and held hands. We realized the significance of this milestone. Riding the two-wheeler helped Julie grow more independent and less dependent on us. She'll now go faster and farther than she's ever gone before. With this growing freedom comes responsibility. Now comes, "Ride only on the sidewalk," "Watch out for younger children," "Look for cars backing out of driveways."

I wanted to explain the whole plan to her: "Later, you'll be allowed to ride in the street. You'll ride friends on the back of your bike. You'll be responsible to let me know where you're going, with whom, and when you'll come home.

"As you learn to be independent, I pray you'll learn to depend not on your own strength, but in the strength the Lord offers. Put your trust in him at all times."

Today, Julie grew toward independence, responsibility, and dependence on God. I envisioned balancing myself responsibly and becoming more like my Father. I trust I'm growing so he's proud of me.

We had survived the first two-wheeler. We knew there would be many such passages ahead: the first day of school, the first school play, the first boyfriend, then (heaven forbid) a driver's license and other such horrors. Each stage would bring us pride because we would train our daughter to accept the responsibilities that accompany each step.

Dear Daughter,

I challenge you not to be a smothering mom, but to let your child's adventuresome spirit have reign, within safety's limits, of course.

Encourage your child with, "Why not? Let's go ahead and try it!" Encourage her to try different things, taste out-of-the-ordinary foods, and touch new things. With each new step, your child will delight you with how she is accepting responsibility. God has designed child rearing so that your child's growing independence comes ever-so-gently; thus, the pain of separation becomes celebration of milestones.

Love, Mom

DEAR LORD,

Place your hedge of protection around my child as she takes her steps out from my safety. Let her little jaunts of independence be successful and bring her confidence. Help me be a mom who will celebrate each victory with her. Let me uplift during the small failures.

In Jesus' name, Amen.

Reflections . . .

God is spirit, and his worshipers must worship in spirit and in truth.

John 4:24

Playing Church

"I get to be the preacher."

"Okay, then I can be the song leader."

The girls had gathered six chairs and lined them up to be their "church." A TV tray was centered up front with graham crackers and little glasses of juice for communion. Julie had on one of her dad's suit coats.

They gathered their dolls, the neighbor boy, and dog Missy to be the congregation. Then the song leader pumped her arm healthily and led a rousing "Jesus Loves Me." After they solemnly served communion, the preacher began. As she held up her pink Bible, six-year-old Julie preached for all she was worth, ad libbing the story of baby Jesus in the manger and the wise men bringing presents.

I was invited to come to church next week. Maybe I would like to preach on Zacchaeus, the wee wee man, Julie suggested.

Their rendition of "church" amused me, but I saw the pure hearts of the children. I saw their sincere desire to worship God in their own way, to offer up to him the fruits of their lives. I have no doubt that God accepted their heartfelt devotion as a holy sacrifice to him.

I wonder. Is my worship to him as pure? As holy? As heartfelt? Or, at times, do I merely "play church"?

Dear Daughter,

Dress up and play acting are such charming parts of childhood. I remember that you used to love wearing my long nightgowns with sweaters, necklaces, and high heels. Sometimes I'd let you put on lipstick and eye shadow, too. You were quite a sight.

Playing dress up allows a child to develop imagination and creativity, so have a special box of dress-up clothes your kids can play with. If you don't have anything of your own that you can leave in the box, go to a thrift store and purchase old formals, high heels, hats, and jewelry.

Dress-up time will be a favorite pastime of your kids. (Remember to keep a camera handy so you can take lots of pictures so Dad and the grandparents won't miss the memories.)

Love, Mom

DEAR GOD,

Make my worship to you a daily praise, holy and acceptable to you. May my motives be pure as a child's, an outpouring of gratitude for what you've done for me through Jesus.

In his name, Amen.

Reflections . . .

_____

_____

_____

_____

_____

_____

_____

_____

_____

_____

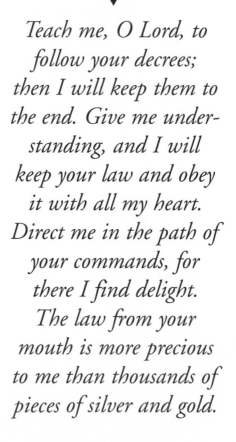

*Teach me, O Lord, to
follow your decrees;
then I will keep them to
the end. Give me under-
standing, and I will
keep your law and obey
it with all my heart.
Direct me in the path of
your commands, for
there I find delight.
The law from your
mouth is more precious
to me than thousands of
pieces of silver and gold.*

Psalm 119:33-35, 72

Dangling Handley

Handley's limp body hung over one of Joy's arms. The cat looked strangled and lifeless, but I noticed that Joy's other hand was tucked under Handley's legs to keep her from being completly strangled. (Partly strangled is a normal state for the cat of a six-year-old.)

They had been out "hunting" in the backyard. Joy, in her tomboy plaid shirt and with a stick for her weapon, and Handley had been stalking the enemy in the tall grass out back. After a long morning of hunting, here came my exhausted troopers in for a snack.

I corrected Joy, "Honey, you're going to hurt Handley carrying her that way. I've told you before, you've got to be gentle with kitty." And, for the hundredth time, I showed her the correct way to hold the cat.

Obediently, Joy hoisted Handley the way I showed her, and they darted off for another adventure.

I don't think Handley cared which end was slung over her owner's arm. Handley, a gift from Joy's gymnastic coach, loyally followed Joy everywhere. They played together, ate together, and slept together. Was it devotion I saw in the kitten's pale blue eyes?

Devotion follows, and faith obeys. Daily, little by little, my faith in my heavenly Father is growing to pattern his unwavering love for me. I am learning to serve my family unselfishly, to put my desires aside for the well-being of others. I'm learning to keep my gossipy mouth shut. I'm getting out of bed quicker for my early quiet time. I'm learning to practice devotion to God, no matter what. No matter how he carries me, no matter where he goes.

Dear Daughter,

You may not feel that you have a deep devotion to God. To you, devotion might seem like an ethereal religious quality, one you're unable to reach.

Au contraire! I want to encourage you to get out your family picture album and browse through it leisurely. Stop and place your finger on every example of devotion you see in those snapshots. You'll probably be surprised at the many faces devotion takes on. You'll realize that you're a leader in devotion, demonstrating to your kids and your husband what practical devotion to God really is.

Keep your camera handy to take lots of pictures of devotion in action in your family. These pictures will encourage you in your spiritual growth through the years.

Love, Mom

DEAR LORD,

Help me to follow. Help me to depend on you for my sustenance. Teach me that I need you for my very life. Teach me to hang on to your every word, to follow you everywhere. It's such a simple lesson, God, but I'm hard of learning. Bless me with devotion.

In Jesus' name, Amen.

Reflections . . .

_____

_____

_____

_____

_____

_____

_____

_____

_____

_____

The Lord your God is with you, he is mighty to save. He will take great delight in you, he will quiet you with his love, he will rejoice over you with singing.

Zephaniah 3:17

Here She Is, Teacher

The night before, we had laid out the new clothes. I had packed the school supplies in the red plaid school tote, and I had planned Julie's favorite breakfast, blueberry pancakes. We fell asleep anticipating the big day, the first day of school.

And now the long-awaited special day had dawned. She was ready! Her curls were caught back perfectly with the new bow. She looked very grownup in her new dress and loafers.

As Julie grabbed her school bag and headed for the car, I noticed how big my little girl had grown, and a lump caught in my throat.

Julie chatted excitedly the whole way to school. She jabbered incessantly about her teacher and the new friends she would make in her class.

Because of the pain in my narrowing throat, I was barely able to utter brief replies to her questions. The view in front of me became blurred and misty. I was in real trouble; I was going to lose it and become one of those first-day-of-school blubbering mothers.

But, the wave of emotion passed. I was going to be okay.

I had long anticipated this "grown-up" day of Julie's. In fact, in my mind I had prepared an introduction of Julie for her teacher. It would go something like this: "This is blue-eyed, blond-haired Julie, one of the two most precious children to me in all this earth. She will be with you from 8:00 A.M.–11:30 A.M., Monday through Friday, though I'm not entirely enthusiastic about the plan.

"Treat her kindly. She's used to getting her way. Talk gently to her. She's used to positive and encouraging words. Teach her to read and write so vistas of challenge and adventure can open up to her. Explain to her why water is clear, worms are gooshy, and giraffes look funny; I've had a hard time with those.

"You may give her extra jobs like straightening chairs, cleaning blackboards, and serving snacks. She excels in pleasing.

"And you have my permission to give Julie lots of hugs. She thrives in a warm, loving atmosphere—like home."

Dear Daughter,

Be on your knees in constant prayer for your child's teacher. Keep communication lines open between you and the teacher with school conferences, informal discussions, and notes. Let him or her know you're an interested and involved parent. Volunteer as much as possible in your child's classroom.

Talk to your child every day about school, especially about his teacher.

All these connections with your child's teacher should help you feel a big part of those school hours. And you'll feel better about turning your child over to someone else for so many hours a day. God will bless your attitude.

Love, Mom

DEAR FATHER,

When I think of turning my daughter over to another person for half the day, I'm scared. Please bless her teacher with gentleness, patience, and wisdom to treat my child as I would—and as you would. Continue to mold my child and me into Christ's image, so you can rejoice over us with singing.

Through Jesus, Amen.

Reflections . . .

◆

I love you, O Lord, my strength. The Lord is my rock, my fortress and my deliverer; my God is my rock, in whom I take refuge. He is my shield and the horn of my salvation, my stronghold.

Psalm 18:1-2

Band-Aids of Compassion

"**M**om-m-m-m-m-eee-eee!" I could tell from the high-pitched scream that Joy was in real pain.

Not sure of the severity of the calamity, I dropped what I was doing and ran outside to the backyard.

There lay Joy on the patio, crumpled over her tricycle in a sad little heap. Her lower lip trembled, and she was trying very hard not to cry, but tears washed her face. She sobbed, "Mommy, I'm hurt bad. Better get the Band-Aids."

The skinned knee was not terminal, and she allowed me to cover the injury with a Band-Aid. Then we added another Band-Aid to yesterday's scrape and one to last week's scratch. And another over a little ache in her finger.

After a little rocking, tear drying, and one more Band-Aid applied to her elbow's phantom pain, Joy calmed down, jumped down, and mounted her bike again, ready to conquer.

All she had needed was some loving and the comfort a Band-Aid gives. Those applied Band-Aids said, "Mom's here. It's going to be okay. Here, let me rock you. Lay your head down. Yes, that's better."

When life's challenges batter me and I'm knocked from my security, do I cry out for my heavenly Father? Like a little child in pain, let me call for my heavenly Father. I learn to open my heart in prayer, turning to God for love and comfort. I listen to his calming words in Scripture; they're like Band-Aids to me. He assures me that I'm in his care, and it will all be okay. Sometimes he sends dear friends to put their arms around me, to tell me they've been there before, that it will work out just fine.

Sometimes God speaks to me in quiet times when I sit and wait for his soothing reassurance. He has never failed me.

Often he sends calming words in the midst of my daily rush. "Slow down," he urges. "I am your anchor. I am enough."

I feel I'm rocking in his arms. He's putting on the Band-Aids and saying, "It'll be all right, my child."

Dear Daughter,

I remember a story about little Janie whose best friend was upset because her doll broke. Because Janie was comforting her sad friend, she was late getting home. Janie's mom asked why she was late, and Janie replied, "Kelly's doll broke."

Mom said, "Oh, did you help her fix it."

"No," replied Janie, "But I helped her cry."

Showing Jesus' compassion may be just that simple. We can be Band-Aids for someone in pain. With your listening ear, gentle touch, kind cards, and patient serving, you model compassion in your family and to those you meet. Your children will easily learn that godly trait of compassion from you. It's true that children will copy what you do, not what you say.

Love, Mom

O GOD,

You alone are my rock and my anchor. When I'm knocked off center, I know you'll be there ready to hold me in comfort.

Give me the strength to be that kind of help for my children. But let me teach them that You alone are our God, our awesome God, the first one we turn to in time of need.

In Jesus' name, Amen.

Reflections . . .

But from everlasting to everlasting the Lord's love is with those who fear him, and his righteousness with their children's children—with those who keep his covenant and remember to obey his precepts.

Psalm 103:17-18

I wait for your salvation, O Lord, and I follow your commands. I obey your statutes, for I love them greatly. I obey your precepts and your statutes, for all my ways are known to you.

Psalm 119:166-168

Willing to Jump

As I tucked Julie in her bed, I noticed that her face was especially contemplative for her six years. Usually she bounced energetically from wall to wall before I could settle her down into the bedtime routine of going to the bathroom, brushing teeth, reading a story, having a drink of water, saying prayers, then, falling asleep (with one more glass of water). Tonight after our prayers, she eyed me seriously as she said, "Mom, I want to get baptized."

"Oh, Julie, that's wonderful! I think that's great, and Jesus is so happy. You can get baptized in a few years when you're older."

I hoped she would understand and would not be too disappointed, but she continued, "No,

Mom, really, I know what it means to get baptized. Don't worry. I'm not afraid. I can do it this Sunday."

The mommy in me just had to say, "Okay, Julie, tell me what it means to get baptized."

"It's when you show Jesus that you can swim. Mom, I know I can do it. Remember, at swimming lessons I could jump in the deep end and swim to you. I know I can do it for Jesus. I can swim all the way across. I'm ready to get baptized! Let's do it this Sunday."

I weasled out of that hip-deep theological discussion as gently as I could by telling her that Jesus was proud of her for wanting to obey, but she would still have to wait a while to learn more about God.

That seemed to satisfy Julie.

Her childlike desire for obedience that she planned to demonstrate on Sunday showed me God's pattern. Julie proclaimed her bold statement of belief and was willing to jump into the water as a sign that she loved Jesus. I commit again to have that obedience to my heavenly Father—to obey, just obey. It's just that simple: obey his commands.

Dear Daughter,

I remember those golden moments of bedtime after the frenzy had calmed down. Take luxurious care at bedtime with your child. She is never more cuddly and loving than when she's had her drink, her story, and her prayers, and she lies in your arms ready to drop off to sleep.

Don't rush these precious moments. Take one more minute to stroke her hair and tell her how special she is to you. Hum a soothing tune. Gently caress her eyelids closed with whispers of how God loves her. Helping her fall asleep in love and security will make for a great disposition tomorrow — hers and yours!

Love, Mom

DEAR GOD,

You give us gifts of little ones to show us the way. Help me to see clearly the eternal lessons my child is teaching me about obedience.

Give me an obedient heart as I learn more and more from your word.

In Jesus' name, Amen.

Reflections . . .

_____

_____

_____

_____

_____

_____

_____

_____

_____

_____

◆

We do not lose heart. Though outwardly we are wasting away, yet inwardly we are being renewed day by day. For our light and momentary troubles are achieving for us an eternal glory that far outweighs them all. So we fix our eyes not on what is seen, but on what is unseen. For what is seen is temporary, but what is unseen is eternal.

2 Corinthians 4:16-18

We All Have Our Hard Chips

We had been in the car for two days, headed home to Grandma's for Christmas. We were tired and nerves were on edge, but we still had another half day's drive.

Six-year-old Joy and eight-year-old Julie fussed over which side of the car was best, whose turn was next, who had the best coloring book, who colored the best, and who was breathing whose air—the usual vacation baggage!

Julie complained for what seemed like the one hundredth time that her sister kept touching her and would I make her keep her hands to herself. She continued to expound on the liabilities of having a little sister, how she was always in the way, always getting her way, always in her stuff, always taking her stuff, always breaking her stuff . . .

Her comments were not very welcome, mainly because we had been cooped up in the car for two days listening to complaints and refereeing fights. Oh, the joy of family vacations!

My terse reply to her tirade: "Julie, we all have our hardships in life." Profound, I thought. Good philosophy for an eight-year-old to chew on for half a day.

Joy reached down from under the seat and pulled up a bag of corn chips and said, "Mom, here are some hard chips. Are these the ones you're talking about? Do you want some?"

Her comments broke the tension, and we laughed for about five miles. After that cleansing laugh, I decided that our hardships weren't so great after all.

I thanked God that I had healthy, bright kids, a loving husband, a car, money for a trip, and a family awaiting us half a day away.

No, we didn't have many hardships.

Dear Daughter,

When I philosophized about hardships in life (and was ready to launch into a treatise on "The Meaning of Life"), all my child heard was corn chips. Face it: kids' perspectives are different from parents' perspectives.

Don't assume that your child sees things the way you see them. Conversation is the window to understanding. For feelings to be understood, ask your child questions and get the words flowing.

There may be times you'll want to slam shut the floodgates of conversation, but, overall, it's great to be known as a mom the kids can say anything to. You may have to practice breathing normally, simply nodding, and not looking surprised when they lay a shocker on you. Trust me, it'll be worth it.

Love, Mom

DEAR LORD,

Give me a sweet attitude to see the bright side of things, and let me not be a complainer. Help me to realize that my hardships can be opportunities for growth and blessing. Let me lean on you.

In Jesus' name, Amen.

Reflections . . .

◆

*Every good and perfect
gift is from above,
coming down from the
Father of the heavenly
lights, who does not
change like shifting
shadows. He chose to
give us birth through
the word of truth,
that we might be a
kind of firstfruits
of all he created.*

James 1:17-18

We Have These Moments

We were on the eighth floor of Oakview General. Looking out the window, we saw people scurrying to their destination and traffic moving along the streets. Life went on at its regular frantic pace.

But not our world. Joy, our nine-year-old, had just been diagnosed with spinal meningitis. We could only stand and watch over her limp body with a 105-degree fever. Our world stood still.

Busy schedules didn't matter. Friends were caring for our older child. Our parents were on their way. We focused on our daughter's tiny body. She looked so small, pale, and helpless lying there in that big bed. I watched the doctors and nurses rush around, and I felt utterly helpless to do anything physical for my daughter .

I knew I could help in other ways. My every whisper became a prayer. "Oh, dear God, let her be all right." In between conversations with my husband and the doctors and nurses, the prayer was on my lips. "Oh, Lord, please let her get well."

Another X ray, a catscan, more blood work. "Please, God."

My prayers became part of me. They were the breaths I took. In—a prayer. Out—a prayer. Like a helpless child, I whispered constantly to my heavenly Father.

As I watched my child, too weak to fight the illness, too weak to ask for a drink of water, I tried to rally my human strength, but nothing surfaced. I realized that I had no control, no choice but to let God be in control. Out of my emptiness, God brought to my mind his promises and his desire for me to claim them. My prayers filled me with his power, and my confidence came from the Lord. I knew it would be all right, that whatever happened would be all right. As I prayed, I waited for the Lord's hand.

After ten days the fever subsided, and Joy was on the road to full recovery. Her illness brought to me a deeper realization that I must turn loose of my own feeble strength and trust the plan of my heavenly Father, whatever it is. Through foggy memories of those ten days in the hospital, I remember the powerful connection I felt with God. I'm beginning to understand some of the complexities of being a parent and how much I need my God.

Dear Daughter,

In the hospital, I was fearful that I might not get to hear more laughter and see more smiles and wipe more tears from my child's face. I felt I hadn't appreciated the good times — the simple, good family times. I felt I was lucky to get a second chance with my child, so I resolved to savor every moment and use eternal eyes to view my family.

An eternal attitude helps when the orange juice spills and the puppy puddles or when your husband doesn't notice you. So, my advice to you is to enjoy the good times. Enjoy each moment fully and thank God for it.

Love, Mom

THANK YOU, GOD

Thank you for the times of affirmation when I feel for sure that you are there. Those times build my faith and help me walk with greater confidence of your care.

In Jesus' name, Amen.

Reflections . . .

_____

_____

_____

_____

_____

_____

_____

_____

_____

_____

_____

All Scripture is God-breathed and is useful for teaching, rebuking, correcting and training in righteousness, so that the man of God may be thoroughly equipped for every good work.

2 Timothy 3:16-17

Fighting the Indians

Julie and her buddy Jake hauled out half of the toys, boxes, blankets, and other assorted paraphernalia from Julie's room and the family room.

"Hey," I called. "Where are you going with all that stuff?"

"We gotta build a fort, Mom. We'll put it all back—honest."

After painstaking construction (and lots of clothespins), they were safely holed up from the attacking Indians.

I noticed that Joy had walked up and tried to join them. I could see the big fight beginning, only this one wouldn't be against the Indians. But wait! They let Joy in the fort. I couldn't believe my eyes.

They settled her safely in one corner and told her sternly to sit there and be quiet, and that they would protect her from the Indians.

The kids battled fiercely for several minutes, appearing to hold the bulwark securely. They were totally absorbed in their make-believe world. Occasionally, I would hear them say, "Joy, get down. The Indians will get you."

And Joy obeyed, enjoying the thrill of battle. But before long she tired of the nine-year-olds' game and slipped out under a back blanket to join me in the house for a kids' show on TV.

I told Julie later that night (after I had cleaned up the fort) how proud I was to see her let her little sister play with her and Jake, how pleased I was to see her want to protect little sister from the Indians.

She took it all in stride and said, "Aw, Mom, someone's got to protect Joy. It might as well be me."

I hope that's a theory she practices for life. That day Julie took a giant step toward maturity in feeling protective toward her little sister. Being kind to a little sister often requires excruciating persistence, but I felt Julie was on her way.

Dear Daughter,

God's word is our strength to act like a Christian. As you learn from God's Word, teach your children the Scriptures so they may learn the attitudes and actions God smiles on.

A friend of mine had been diligently teaching her children to memorize verses of Scripture and use them as swords against the devil, but she doubted that any of it was sinking in. One day, however, she got a sign from God.

Morgan, her four-year-old, had been fussy and difficult, so my friend asked her daughter, "Morgan, is the devil trying to make you cranky and fussy?"

A light must have gone off in Morgan's head because she swung her imaginary sword and declared in her loudest fighting voice, "Rejoice in the Lord always, and again I say rejoice."

Instill the words of the Lord in your children, so they can use them when they need them. The Lord will bring the blessing.   Love, Mom

DEAR GOD,

Help me notice each bit of progress my kids make toward growing in the Christian virtues. Nudge me to encourage and praise them earnestly for their good works.

In Jesus' name, Amen.

Reflections . . .

*O Lord, you are
our Father.
We are the clay,
you are the potter;
we are all the work
of your hand.*

Isaiah 64:8

Be Yielded

J oy watched me working at my potter's wheel. I quickly formed the sides of the pot, then flared them out to make a large salad bowl.

"Let me have a turn, Mom. Can I try making a pot?"

"Sure, you can." But I thought, it's harder than it looks, Joy.

Ten-year-old Joy sat down at my wheel. I showed her how to pat the clay in a ball and slam it down on the potter's wheel. She put her hands on the spinning wet clay and laughed.

"O-o-oh. It's gooshy! Feels neat-o!" Her hands and arms, even her body, bumped from the force of the off-center clay. I tried to guide her hands to center the clay. Try as she would, she wasn't strong enough to center the clay and make her pot.

She lacked patience, too. In just a few minutes, she jumped up and announced, "I'm through. Gotta go to Courtney's and ride bikes. You can finish, Mom."

As I worked at the wheel finishing her pot, I thought of how God is the master potter and of how he has his hands on me, molding and making me into the wife and mother he wants me to be.

Am I yielded to his hands?

As the master potter, God has ultimate patience as he forms me daily into his useful vessel. He quietly works on me when I'm stubborn and resist his molding. He knows what is best, sometimes trimming, pruning, or reshaping as necessary to turn out a finished product of glory.

God knows that pots must be fired to become hardened and useful for service. I may not understand why I must go through the fire of the kiln, but God knows what is best. Later the pot must be glazed, another painful process but one that is necessary for usefulness, beauty, and lasting value.

My job is to be yielded to God's touch and to let the master potter have his own way with me.

Dear Daughter,

Your children may have completely different interests from yours, but that's okay. Rather than being disappointed that you girls didn't become potters, I tried to expose you to several interests and hobbies, so you could find out what you did enjoy.

If your children don't show an inclination toward sports, show them art, and let them try drawing or painting. Let your children experience lots of different hobbies. Take them to museums, libraries, shops, and craft shows where their horizons can be broadened. Realize, too, that their interests may go in cycles, like the phases of the moon. Encourage them to try an activity a second or third time before switching their focus.

Show your enthusiasm for new ways of doing things. It'll rub off on your kids. I pray for you daily, dear daughter, that your mothering will be as fun and full as mine has been. Remember to let your kids be your delight, and remember to be a silly mom.

Love, Mom

DEAR GOD,

Teach me to be content and to be yielded to your working in my life and the lives of my chidren. Let me not jump off the potter's wheel and run off in my own direction, but let me wait patiently on you.

Help me teach this calm assurance to my children. In Jesus' name, Amen.

Reflections . . .

Find rest, O my soul, in God alone; my hope comes from him. He alone is my rock and my salvation; he is my fortress, I will not be shaken. My salvation and my honor depend on God; he is my mighty rock, my refuge. Trust in him at all times, O people; pour out your hearts to him, for God is our refuge.

Psalm 62:5-8

"Can You, Mom, Huh?"

"**M**om," Julie said as soon as I walked in the door, "My teacher wants you to be room mother for my class. I told her I thought you would. Can you, huh, can you?"

"Whew," I sighed, setting down my briefcase and kicking off my shoes. My first words were almost, "You know I work full-time," but instead I managed, "Tell me about it."

"Mrs. Ellis says fifth grade gets three parties this year, and they're really going to be neat. We'll have a Christmas party and a Valentine party and an end-of-school party. We need a mom to serve cookies and punch. I told Mrs. Ellis that you baked yummy cookies and that you'd be the best room mother. I really want you to do it, Mom. It'd be so neat having you at my school. Ple-e-e-ze!"

I couldn't stop her excitement or her words. I learned that the room mother plans the parties, coordinates other class projects with the teacher, and volunteers every week in the classroom.

I searched long for gentle words, "Honey, you know I work. I'd really like to be at your school for the parties, but I just can't. I'm sorry."

My heart ached because I knew how my reply disappointed her. I caught only a glimpse of the rejection in her eyes. She looked at the ground and her lip quivered a bit. "Oh, that's okay, Mom."

In addition to the stress of juggling the girls' after-school activities and rides, arranging proper supervision, my full-time job outside the home, and my full-time job in the home, the guilt overwhelms me. It's always there, tempting me with thoughts of insecurity, whispering that I'm not a good mom, that I don't do enough.

Hoping I could ease her pain a little, I explained to Julie that she and I would bake some special cookies for her parties. I could come up to school sometimes to join her for lunch in the cafeteria. I asked her if she'd like to take a day off school and come stay all day with me at my office.

"Oh, Mom, could I? That'd be so cool!"

"Sure, we'll talk to Mrs. Ellis and ask when would be a good time. You can take your homework and study at my office. And we'll go out to lunch with some of my friends. I think you'll like them."

Dear Daughter,

If you're a work-outside-the-home mom, you may find the stress overwhelming at times. But know that you can handle whatever pressures come your way because you look to the Lord for strength.

You may have to get up a little earlier to spend time with the Lord. You will have to plan carefully to juggle schedules and the sharing of household tasks.

Let your family know that although you have outside commitments, your husband and kids are number one. Include them as often as possible in your work activities.

Make your time at home all theirs; don't bring work home.

If you stay at home with your children, don't believe the worldly lies that you must work outside the home to have worth. Know that mothering is one of the highest callings of the Lord, an occupation of noble value, ordained by God.

Love, Mom

DEAR LORD,

You know the torment of my heart and the guilt I deal with daily. Whisper your words of assurance to me. Ease my mind. Let me know you can help me juggle wisely. Let me give my family first place in my heart.

In Jesus' name, Amen.

Reflections . . .

*For my thoughts are
not your thoughts,
neither are your
ways my ways,
declares the Lord.
As the heavens are
higher than the
earth, so are my
ways higher than
your ways and my
thoughts than your
thoughts.*

Isaiah 55:8-9

Gorillas on the Windshield

"I t's really cold, Mom, what's the windshield's temperature today?"

Driving home from church, we shivered from freezing temperatures as we waited for the car heater to warm up. I wondered why Joy wanted to know the temperature of the windshield. Who can fathom the thoughts of a twelve-year-old girl? I bravely ventured a question:

"What do you mean, the windshield's temperature? Why do you want to know how cold the windshield is?"

Joy explained how the news weathercasters always gave the windshield factor in the weather report. She assumed the temperature of the windshield played great significance in the weather conditions. Since tonight was particularly cold, she was curious about the windshield's temperature.

It finally hit me! She had misunderstood the weathermen all these years to say "windshield factor" when they were saying "wind chill factor." I tried not to laugh at Joy's misguided comprehension and explained "wind chill factor" to her. I reveled in the moment as I imparted new information to my child. I realized my moments of intellect were coming fewer and farther between, and soon, as my daughter reached teenage years, my intellect would quietly slip into oblivion, as it does with most parents. But it was comforting to know that for this moment, my child was anxious to listen.

Joy was appreciative of my wisdom and, in fact, encouraged me with, "Mom, there's another thing I've always wondered about. Gorilla warfare has always worried me. I mean, in all these wars, when soldiers are fighting and everything, wouldn't they be afraid with all those gorillas out there fighting, too? Wouldn't the gorillas attack the soldiers? Gee, I'd be afraid if gorillas were around me. Can't they do anything about the gorillas?"

I felt more confident this time with a dictionary lesson and a spelling drill. I chuckled, and Joy laughed at her dim understanding and was quite happy with her new-found information.

I knew her questions would not always be so easy to answer. There were teen years ahead, full of exciting challenges when she might not welcome my input. So I thanked God that I was here to explain the easy ones, like wind chill factor and guerilla warfare.

Dear Daughter,

In my generation, statistics proved that moms had the greatest influence over their children's faith. However, in our changing world with its violence, crime, and brokenness, we can feel overwhelmed and helpless. But when I consider what kind of mother you'll be, I'm comforted and reassured. You and your friends who are moms will still be the most positive influences on your kids' religious faith. Teach your kids the ways of God.

Keep the communication lines open for the questions your youngsters want to ask. Take time for each question, no matter how small or silly. There may be a profound lesson waiting to be learned.

Let your child know you have all the time in the world for him and his questions. Turn off the T.V., take the phone off the hook for a minute, look your child in the eye, and listen. God will miraculously bless you with the right words. And remember, sometimes the right words are "I don't know. Let's find out together."

Don't let anyone tell you that your job isn't important or that you should get out in the workplace and get a "real" job. Know that your job of mothering is of utmost importance. Your kids really need you. It's true.

Love, Mom

DEAR GOD,

Though your ways are higher than mine, I thank you for giving me the understanding I need to be a great mom. Continue to prick my heart to ask. I know you will be faithful to give, as you've promised. Help me teach your ways to my children.

In Jesus' name, Amen.

Reflections . . .

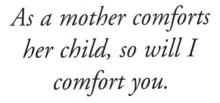

*As a mother comforts
her child, so will I
comfort you.*

Isaiah 66:13

That Must Really Hurt

Julie's countenance had fallen. Indeed, it dragged on the floor as she came in the door. I knew before she spoke the dreaded words, "Mom, I lost the election."

She plopped down on the couch, ready to cry, but trying hard not to. "Chad won."

We had been up late all week making posters that said, "Vote for Julie for Eighth Grade President." We'd used huge letters with bold colors; we'd even added glitter and curly ribbon to attract attention. Julie's enthusiasm had spilled over into my attitude, and I had begun to believe, even know, that she would win. The harder we had worked, the more I had believed it.

So the news Julie brought home shocked me. The disappointment settled over me, too, as I sat on the couch with my daughter.

"That must hurt worse than anything else in the world."

"Mom, I can't believe it! Everyone said they voted for me!"

We sat for several minutes. No words. Just silent communication of "It really hurts." Then I left her alone.

I wondered at the time if I was doing the right thing or if I was doing enough, but later Julie told me that not talking about the election at that moment was the perfect thing to do. She needed her space and time alone to deal with the defeat. She knew that I understood the gravity of the pain. That was enough. Helping her know I was willing to share her pain was a first step, an open door. I wanted to soothe her, to defend her, to make her feel better; but like dealing with grief, only Julie could deal with her own hurt.

I didn't want my child to have to endure pain, any pain (that's why we're so good at passing out aspirin and cough syrup). I'd bear it all for her if I could, but then, how would my child learn and grow? Though the mom in me wanted to cure Julie's problem, I could only let her know that I cared.

Dear Daughter,

Sometimes the best comfort for a child who has failed is "That must really hurt." Avoid saying, "It'll be all right." "Don't cry." "You'll feel better tomorrow." "Look on the bright side." The immediate pain is so intense that your child may feel it will never be all right again. So don't make light of the situation, your child may feel that you're denying her pain.

Later, you can share times you failed: when you lost the election or failed algebra or set the tea pot on fire.

There may be times you can comfort her by telling her that God has something good in mind for her, but it's not being class president right now.

Remember, she isn't looking for you to fix her predicament or offer advice. She needs you to identify with her loss, acknowledge its heaviness, and bear a little with her. I know you can do it.

Love, Mom

DEAR LORD,

When I feel so empty and low, remind me that you are my Father who understands the pain and loneliness. You allowed your son to suffer great pain and loneliness for me. Help me to live appreciatively.

In Jesus' name, Amen.

*R*eflections . . .

_____

_____

_____

_____

_____

_____

_____

_____

_____

_____

_____

_____

Good and upright is the Lord; therefore he instructs sinners in his ways. He guides the humble in what is right and teaches them his way. All the ways of the Lord are loving and faithful for those who keep the demands of his covenant. For the sake of your name, O Lord, forgive my iniquity, though it is great.

Psalm 25:8-11

Sweet Forgiveness

Almost as soon as the words exploded from my mouth, I wished I could take them back.

Joy and her friends had bounded into the house, excited that their school had won the football game, and I sarcastically commented on her not cleaning her room before she left as she had promised.

Joy fixed her eyes on me. At first she looked paralyzed, then like she wanted to shrink into the carpet. Her eyes said she wished I would evaporate from this planet. A painful stab in my heart told me my mistake. I tried to cut the tension in the room with a light-hearted comment, but I could see it was too late.

After the friends left, Joy retreated to her room. The slamming door signaled me that my misdeed was greater than I first thought.

I felt like defending myself. I wanted to explain that she had promised to clean her room before she left for the game, that I was only pointing out that she had broken her promise. I could have grounded her or taken away the phone, but I didn't. On and on . . . I wanted to justify my behavior, but the bottom line was: I was wrong. There was only one thing to do.

I knocked on her door, went in, and sat down on the bed by her. "Joy, I'm sorry. I shouldn't have corrected you in front of your friends. I was wrong. I'm sorry."

Simple words. No rationalization. Just an apology.

Joy responded with grace, "Oh, it's all right, Mom. It's no big deal."

Sweet, simple words of forgiveness. Her soothing words helped my struggle. If only I could forgive myself as easily. We moms try so hard to do right, to be perfect, to make our families perfect. We fail so often.

Why do we have so much trouble accepting and admitting our shortcomings? Maybe down deep inside I feel I won't be honored and respected if I confess my failures. I fear I would fall in the eyes of my children. But only when I admit my faults will my girls learn how to handle their own failures. If I were perfect, would my daughters feel a need for God?

Dear Daughter,

Correcting and disciplining is your God-given lot as a mom, but do not correct your children in front of their friends, especially as your kids get older—preteen and up.

Your kids have worked hard for respect from their friends. It is an unwise mom who erodes that respect lightly. Any belittling of your kids in front of their peers tears down your kids' self-esteem and the respect of their friends. You will tear yourself down a notch in everyone's eye.

If correction is absolutely necessary at the moment, take your child aside and privately talk to her about the problem. A lengthy discussion can be continued later, after the friends have gone home.

Always honor your kids in front of their friends. Use positive, happy words to create an atmosphere of acceptance. You want to have a home that your kids will want to bring their friends to.

Love, Mom

DEAR LORD,

Help me to be transparent to my family, to show my true self. I don't want to be known as a perfect "Super Mom" who can't relate to weakness.

I want to confess to you and to my family, so you can cleanse me and strengthen me. Help me set the pattern for my kids.

In Jesus' name, Amen.

Reflections . . .

_____

_____

_____

_____

_____

_____

_____

_____

_____

◆

*His compassions
never fail. They
are new every
morning; great is
your faithfulness.*

Lamentations 3:22b-23

Passed With Flying Colors

I sat in the car waiting. I read my book and waited some more. I listened to the radio news and waited some more. I prayed and waited some more. I tried reading my book again, and waited still. My nerves were agitated as I waited, wondering, "Would she pass?"

As Joy bounded out of the driver's license office, her smile said it all. "Yea! I passed," she screamed. Our sixteen-year-old was now a licensed driver. I felt excited for her, aware that new adventures awaited her, but my heart said, "Ugh."

Not wanting to squelch her enthusiasm, I giggled with her, "Oh, I just can't believe it! You're driving now! Wow! How neat!" She drove me home. The next day she was off on her own with books and lunch money, going to school, alone in the car.

I dragged into the house with my own motherly "baggage." How could it be? This child I gave birth to only a few years ago had taken off alone in the car. Again, another leaving-the-nest milestone, another step toward maturity, a step I screamed out against. I wasn't ready for a child old enough to drive!

In my quiet bedroom, I sank to my knees and bowed my head on the bed. I don't often pray out loud, but this time I couldn't stop my outburst. I felt like a fearful, helpless child crying in the dark for her daddy. I couldn't hold back my tears, so they flowed as I prayed.

Though Joy was an adult in the eyes of many and could now legally drive, I explained to God the special care she needed.

"God, Joy isn't a very experienced driver, so her reflexes might be slow. Please, don't let anyone stop suddenly in front of her. Please, Father, don't let the sun shine directly in her eyes as she's behind the wheel, because she might not think to slow down. Don't let a truck and trailer turn left in front of her; she might not be able to judge its speed. Help her keep her eyes on the road and off the radio buttons. Help her drive defensively, not meditatively."

I felt better after I had poured out my heart to God. I know he didn't need my explanations, but his graceful cleansing covered me.

We moms often have callouses on our knees from being in prayer for our children. Oh, how we need the Father's help to keep us and our children on the right road.

Dear Daughter,

Treasure these things in your heart, as the mother of Jesus did. Each stage is unique and precious and contains special memories to value. I remember how each new "trick" you did was the biggest and best. I'd brag to whomever would listen—my friends at church, my mom, the grocery clerk, the bank teller— about how advanced you were. I may have been too anxious to "encourage" you to the next exciting stage.

Before I realized it, you were eating real food, walking, talking, riding a bike, heading for school, driving, going to college, then marrying. Now I wonder: "Where'd the time go?"

Slow down, honey, and treasure these moments. Laugh more and be a silly mom!

Love, Mom

DEAR GOD,

Let your angels of protection surround my child as she ventures out on her own toward independence—be they tiny, halting steps or giant, determined ones. Help her to honor the trust we have placed in her. Keep our training fresh in her mind. Let her not stray from your paths. Though these steps of independence are hard for me to accept, I know they're normal stages of development, and I really wouldn't have it any other way. Lord, let your compassion be full towards my family; I claim your promises.

In Jesus' name, Amen.

*R*eflections . . .